EVEN POETS DANCE

Morten E. Fadum

MAZURI PRESS

Request for permission should be submit-
ted to Morten Fadum, Mazuri Press, 2118
Paulsen Rd., Harvard, Illinois 60033.

Printed and bound by
Worzalla Publishing Co.
Stevens Point, Wisconsin,
for Mazuri Press in a second
edition of 2000 copies
October, 1998.

MAZURI PRESS

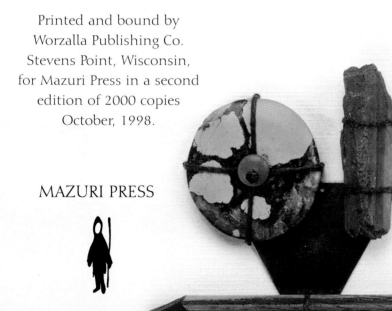

For Jemma
"Born by a mother
with a dancer's heart."

ISBN 0-9651148-0-5

AT THE EDGE OF THE WOODS
CLOSE TO OUR HOME
WHERE MY DAUGHTER HAS TAKEN TO PLAY
IS A PLACE FROM A TIME
SO LONG AGO

WHEN DEVILS WERE DANCING AWAY

DANCE TO THE MOTHERS SONG
A CHILD IS BORN
WHEN THE DANCE
IS DONE

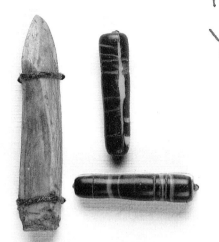

I SAW YOU IN THE WINDOW
YOUR HEAD UPON A PILLOW
WITH SUNLIGHT
GENTLY WARMING
THE THINGS
YOU HOLD INSIDE

LISTEN TO THE SELF

HE IS A LEADER
    IN ALL THINGS
BUT WHEN HE WAS
        YOUNG
HE WAS SUCH A WILD
        BOY

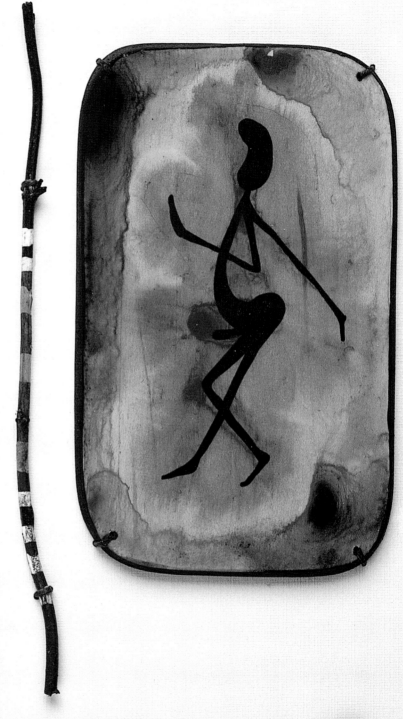

ON THE RIVER
AND OUT OF THE MIST
WE GAVE DEATH AND DANCING
        EQUAL PLACE

NO ONE ASKED FOR LESS
IT WAS A GREAT ADVENTURE

RUN WITH WOLVES
IF YOU MUST
BUT WHEN YOU SLEEP
SLEEP LIGHTLY

WE CARRY THE IMAGE
OF A DANCERS DREAM
WHAT TALE THE DANCES TELL

LAY DOWN YOUR SWORD
AND STEP AWAY
FROM THX CHILD

I HAVE SEEN
   THE THREE MAIDENS
THEY COME WITH THE MIST
TO CARRY CHILDREN
   FROM DANGER
TO COMFORT WOMEN
   IN PAIN
FEEL THEIR TOUCH
   WHEN YOU'RE SLEEPING

THEIRS IS AN OLD SONG

SHE SHOWED NO fEAR
WHEN THE BATTLE CAME

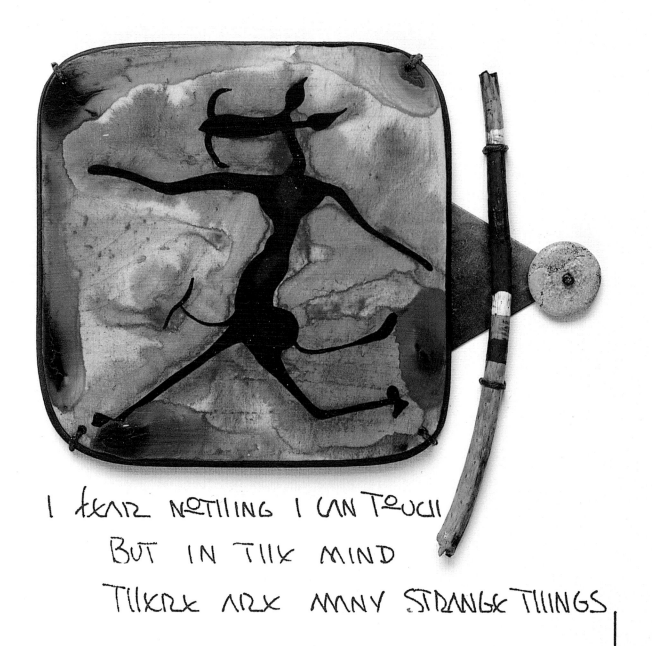

I fear nothing I can touch
But in the mind
There are many strange things

THERE IS A STRUGGLE
    IN ALL of US
THIS IS THE WAY IT HAS ALWAYS BEEN

WE ARE A SERIES
OF SMALL
COINCIDENCES

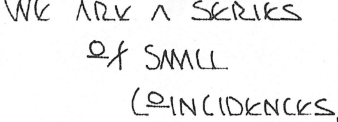

WE FEASTED
ON HIS STRENGTH
AND SLEPT
WITH HIS DREAMS
THE WOLVES CAME
AND WE ROSE TO HUNT
AGAIN

WISDOM CAME
AND THE PEOPLE
RAN
THEY HIDE
FOR A THOUSAND
YEARS

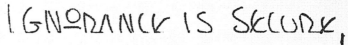

IGNORANCE IS SECURE

IF A KING
OFFERS TO GIVE YOU
HIS DAUGHTER
JUST FOR SAVING
A CASTLE

SHOOT THE KING

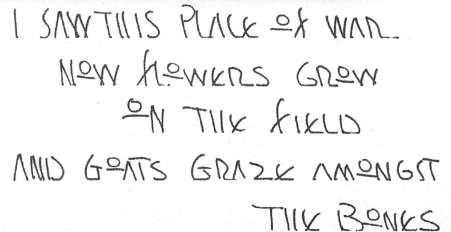

I SAW THIS PLACE OF WAR
NOW FLOWERS GROW
ON THE FIELD
AND GOATS GRAZE AMONGST
THE BONES

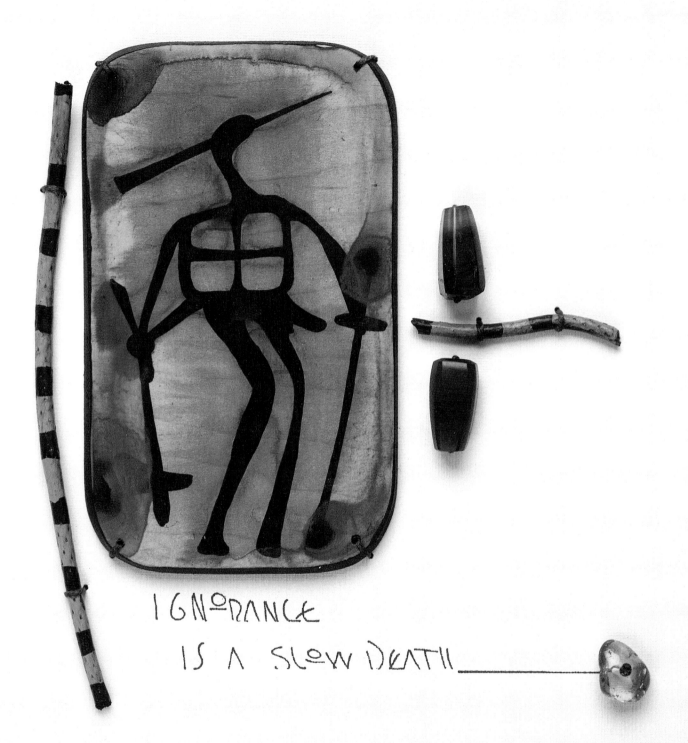

IGNORANCE
IS A SLOW DEATH

WHEN THE
LAST WARRIOR
DIED
THE WOMEN
BURIED
THE WEAPONS
AND CARRIED
THE CHILDREN
AWAY

CARE FOR THE CHILD PLACE
IT IS SAFE AS IT IS WISE

I AM THE HUMAN
THAT LIVES
ON THE EDGE OF THE FOREST

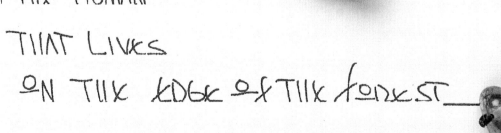

I found a place

 where a warrior died

when we were children

we played games of battle

we will never be children

 again

and battle never a game_____

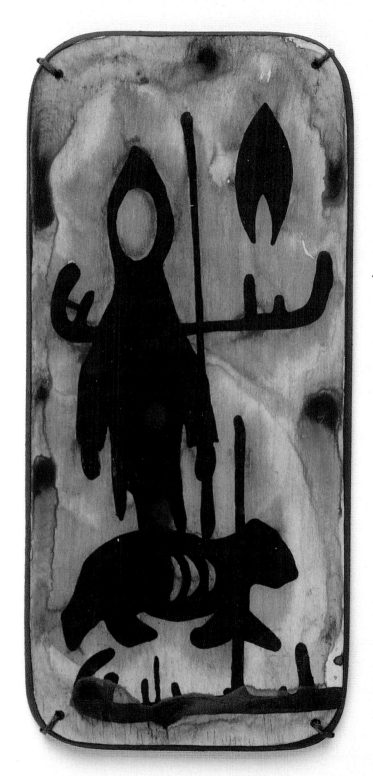

READING
THE THUNDER...
AND THE
RUSTLING
OF LEAVES
I AM
A TRAVELER

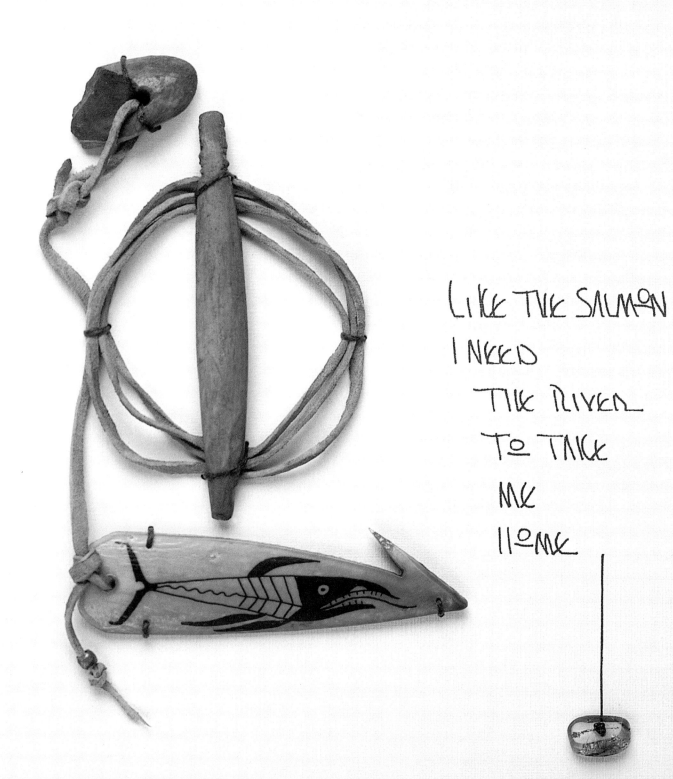

LIKE THE SALMON
I NEED
THE RIVER
TO TAKE
ME
HOME

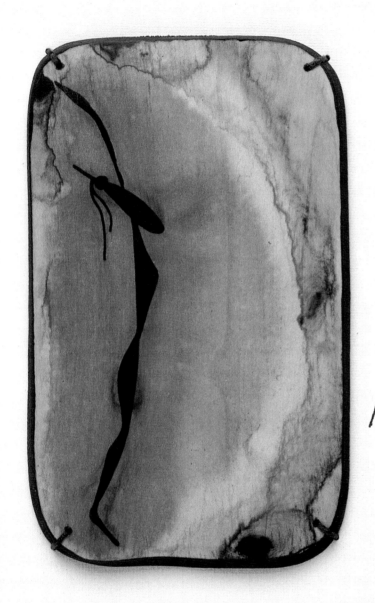

SIIK IS
ON TIIK BOUNDRY
AND WAITING
FOR CHANGE
ANCIENT

AND FOREVER YOUNG

I SAW YOU
FROM MY
DREAMING
TREE

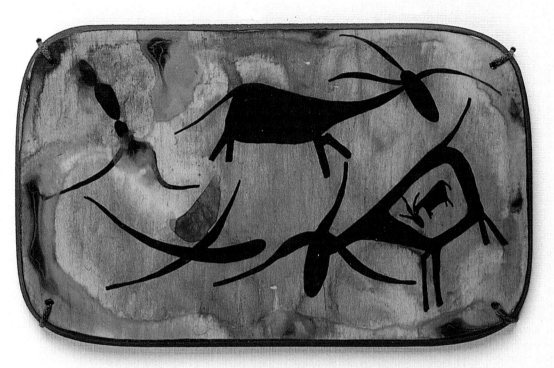

CARE FOR THE BEAST
IIK IS PART OF YOU

SHE IS THE BEAR
KEEPER OF DREAMS
ENTER HER CAVE
WITH EMPTY HANDS
AND SHE GREETS YOU

I AM HER LOVER
    SHE IS MY DANCER.

WE ARE THE KEEPERS OF A HEART _____